Navigating the Education System A Student's Guide to Educational Leadership and Policy

Desmond Titus

Copyright © [2023]

Title: Navigating the Education System A Student's Guide to Educational Leadership and Policy
Author's: Desmond Titus

This book was printed and published by [Publisher's: **Desmond Titus**] in [2023]

ISBN

TABLE OF CONTENT

Chapter 4: Education Policies and Their Impact

Introduction to Education Policies

Analyzing the Impact of Policies on Students

Examining Policy Implementation Challenges

Chapter 5: Student Advocacy and Leadership

Empowering Students to Become Advocates

Developing Leadership Skills in Education

Strategies for Effectively Communicating with Education Authorities

Chapter 6: Educational Policy Development

The Process of Policy Development

Identifying and Addressing Education System Issues

Engaging Students in Policy Discussions and Decision-Making

Chapter 10: Navigating Career Paths in Educational Leadership

Exploring Career Opportunities in Educational Leadership

Building the Skills and Qualifications for Leadership Roles

Networking and Professional Development Opportunities

Chapter 11: Conclusion

Reflecting on the Journey of Navigating the Education System

Key Takeaways and Action Steps for Students in Educational Leadership and Policy

Chapter 1: Introduction to Educational Leadership and Policy

Understanding the Importance of Educational Leadership

In today's rapidly evolving world, the role of educational leadership has become increasingly crucial. Educational leaders are the driving force behind the development and implementation of policies and practices that shape the education system. As students, it is essential for us to comprehend the significance of educational leadership and its impact on our learning experiences.

Educational leadership refers to the skills, knowledge, and abilities required to lead educational institutions effectively. It involves a range of responsibilities, including creating a vision for the future, setting goals, making informed decisions, and fostering a positive learning environment. Educational leaders, such as principals, superintendents, and policymakers, play a vital role in shaping the quality of education we receive.

One of the primary reasons why educational leadership is crucial is its ability to drive positive change within the education system. Effective leaders are instrumental in identifying and addressing the various challenges and issues faced by students and educators. By focusing on improving teaching methods, curriculum development, and student support systems, educational leaders can enhance the overall quality of education.

Moreover, educational leadership plays a significant role in promoting equity and social justice within the education system. Leaders who are committed to creating inclusive environments ensure that all students have equal access to resources and opportunities, irrespective of their background or circumstances. By addressing disparities and promoting diversity, educational leaders lay the foundation for a fair and just education system.

Furthermore, educational leadership also influences policy development and implementation. Leaders in this field work closely with policymakers to advocate for policies that benefit students and educators. They provide valuable insights and recommendations based on their experiences and expertise, ensuring that policies are aligned with the needs of students and the broader educational community.

As students, understanding the importance of educational leadership empowers us to actively engage in our education. By recognizing the role educational leaders play in shaping our learning experiences, we can become informed advocates for positive change. We can collaborate with leaders and policymakers, sharing our perspectives, ideas, and concerns, to contribute to the development of effective educational policies.

In conclusion, educational leadership is a critical aspect of the education system that significantly impacts students and educators alike. By understanding its importance, students can actively participate in shaping their educational journey and contribute to the betterment of the education system as a whole.

The Role of Policy in Shaping Education Systems

In today's ever-changing educational landscape, policies play a crucial role in shaping and transforming education systems. It is essential for students, the future leaders and policymakers, to understand the significance of policy in bringing about positive changes in the realm of education. This subchapter will explore the role of policy in shaping education systems and its impact on students.

Education policies serve as guidelines and frameworks that dictate the goals, strategies, and standards of educational institutions. These policies are formulated by educational leaders and policymakers, who consider the needs and aspirations of students, teachers, parents, and the community at large. As students, it is essential to recognize that educational policies are not static; they evolve in response to societal changes, advancements in technology, and emerging global trends.

The impact of educational policies on students is profound. Policies influence various aspects of education, including curriculum design, assessment methods, teaching methodologies, and the overall learning environment. For instance, policies that promote inclusive education ensure that students from diverse backgrounds, including those with disabilities, have equal access to quality education. Policies can also address issues like bullying, mental health support, and career guidance, ensuring a safe and nurturing environment for students.

Understanding educational policy is crucial for students interested in educational leadership and policy. By familiarizing themselves with policies, students can become advocates for change, contributing to the improvement of their educational institutions. Moreover, by engaging with policy discussions, students can have a voice in shaping policies that directly impact their educational journey.

Furthermore, policy literacy empowers students to critically analyze and evaluate policies, identifying their strengths, weaknesses, and potential consequences. This enables students to actively engage in policy debates, propose innovative solutions, and contribute to the development of effective policies. By doing so, students can become agents of change, transforming their educational systems for the betterment of all.

In conclusion, the role of policy in shaping education systems cannot be undermined. As students interested in educational leadership and policy, it is vital to understand the significance of policies in driving educational transformations. By engaging with policy discussions, advocating for change, and critically analyzing policies, students can contribute to the improvement of their educational institutions and create a positive impact on the lives of future generations.

Chapter 2: The Basics of Educational Leadership

Defining Educational Leadership

In today's complex and rapidly changing educational landscape, the role of educational leaders has become increasingly important. Educational leadership refers to the practice of guiding and inspiring individuals, teams, and entire educational institutions to achieve their goals and fulfill their missions. It involves creating a vision, setting goals, making strategic decisions, and implementing effective policies and practices that promote student success and educational excellence.

At its core, educational leadership is about making a positive impact on the lives of students. Educational leaders have a profound influence on the teaching and learning process, shaping the educational experiences of students and creating an environment that fosters their intellectual, social, and emotional growth. They are responsible for creating a safe and inclusive learning environment, ensuring equitable access to quality education, and promoting academic achievement for all students, regardless of their backgrounds or abilities.

Educational leadership is not limited to principals and superintendents; it extends to teachers, counselors, and other professionals who play leadership roles within their classrooms and schools. It is a collaborative and distributed practice that involves building relationships, fostering teamwork, and empowering others to take on leadership responsibilities.

To be an effective educational leader, one must possess a diverse set of skills and qualities. These include strong communication and interpersonal skills, the ability to motivate and inspire others, a deep understanding of educational policies and systems, and a commitment to continuous learning and professional growth. It is also crucial for educational leaders to have a clear understanding of educational policies and their implications, as they often shape the direction and priorities of educational institutions.

Understanding and engaging with educational leadership and policy is vital for students who aspire to become future leaders in the education field. By familiarizing themselves with the principles and practices of educational leadership, students can gain insights into the challenges and opportunities that lie ahead. They can also develop the skills and knowledge necessary to advocate for equitable and inclusive educational practices, contribute to meaningful educational reforms, and make a positive difference in the lives of students.

In this subchapter, we will explore the various dimensions of educational leadership, including the roles and responsibilities of educational leaders, the impact of educational policies on student outcomes, and the essential skills and qualities required for effective leadership. We will delve into the different theories and models of leadership, examine case studies of successful educational leaders, and provide practical tips and advice for students interested in pursuing careers in educational leadership and policy.

Whether you are a student interested in educational leadership or simply curious about the field, this subchapter will serve as a comprehensive guide to understanding and navigating the complexities of educational leadership in today's education system.

Different Leadership Styles in Education

In the realm of education, leadership plays a crucial role in shaping the direction and success of educational institutions. Educational leaders are responsible for creating a positive learning environment, implementing effective policies, and fostering innovation. However, leadership styles can vary greatly, with each style having its strengths and weaknesses. Understanding the different leadership styles in education can empower students to recognize and appreciate the various approaches taken by educational leaders.

1. Transformational Leadership: This leadership style focuses on inspiring and motivating others to achieve their full potential. Transformational leaders encourage creativity, empower students and staff, and foster collaboration. They set high expectations and provide the necessary support to help their team members reach their goals. This style of leadership promotes a positive and innovative learning environment.

2. Transactional Leadership: Transactional leaders focus on setting clear expectations, providing rewards and punishments based on performance, and maintaining order and discipline. They are task-oriented and emphasize compliance with rules and regulations. While this leadership style can be effective in ensuring discipline and order, it may limit creativity and autonomy.

3. Servant Leadership: Servant leaders prioritize the needs of others above their own. They focus on serving their students, teachers, and staff, and aim to foster a supportive and nurturing environment. Servant leaders promote teamwork, empathy, and collaboration. They are committed to the growth and well-being of their educational community.

4. Democratic Leadership: Democratic leaders involve students, staff, and other stakeholders in the decision-making process. They value the input and opinions of others and encourage open communication. This leadership style promotes a sense of ownership and shared responsibility among students and staff.

5. Laissez-Faire Leadership: Laissez-faire leaders adopt a hands-off approach, allowing students and staff to have maximum freedom and autonomy. They provide minimal guidance and direction, instead allowing individuals to make decisions independently. While this style can promote creativity and independence, it may also lead to confusion and lack of accountability.

Understanding these different leadership styles in education can help students navigate their educational journey more effectively. By recognizing the strengths and weaknesses of each style, students can appreciate the efforts of their educational leaders and contribute to a positive learning environment. Additionally, understanding leadership styles can inspire students to develop their own leadership skills and find their unique leadership style in the future.

In conclusion, leadership styles in education vary greatly, each with its own strengths and weaknesses. Transformational, transactional, servant, democratic, and laissez-faire leadership styles all play a significant role in shaping educational institutions. By understanding these different styles, students can develop a deeper appreciation for their educational leaders and gain insight into their own potential as future leaders.

Key Competencies for Effective Educational Leaders

In the ever-evolving landscape of education, the role of educational leaders has become increasingly crucial. These leaders play a vital role in shaping policies, making important decisions, and driving positive change within educational institutions. To be effective in their roles, educational leaders must possess a unique set of competencies that enable them to navigate the complex challenges of the education system.

1. Visionary Leadership: Effective educational leaders have a clear vision for the future of education. They can inspire and motivate others by articulating a compelling vision that aligns with the needs of students, educators, and the community. By setting high expectations and goals, they encourage excellence and innovation in teaching and learning.

2. Communication Skills: Communication is key in any leadership position. Educational leaders must be able to effectively communicate their vision, ideas, and expectations to various stakeholders, including students, parents, teachers, and policymakers. Strong communication skills foster trust, collaboration, and a shared sense of purpose among all involved parties.

3. Ethical Decision-Making: Educational leaders often face complex ethical dilemmas that require them to make difficult decisions. They must possess a strong moral compass and be guided by ethical principles to ensure that their actions prioritize the best interests of students and uphold the values of fairness, equity, and inclusivity.

4. Problem-Solving Abilities: The education system is constantly faced with challenges and obstacles. Effective educational leaders are skilled

problem solvers who can analyze situations, identify root causes, and develop innovative solutions. They encourage a culture of continuous improvement and foster a supportive environment where challenges are seen as opportunities for growth.

5. Collaborative Mindset: Educational leaders recognize the importance of collaboration and teamwork. They actively seek input from various stakeholders, value diverse perspectives, and build strong relationships with others. By fostering a collaborative culture, they create a sense of shared responsibility and empower others to contribute to the improvement of educational practices.

6. Resilience and Adaptability: Educational leaders must be resilient in the face of adversity and able to adapt to changing circumstances. They embrace challenges as learning opportunities, remain positive in the face of setbacks, and demonstrate a growth mindset. Their ability to navigate uncertainty and lead through change is crucial in driving continuous improvement and ensuring the success of all students.

In conclusion, effective educational leaders possess a unique set of key competencies that enable them to navigate the education system successfully. These competencies include visionary leadership, strong communication skills, ethical decision-making, problem-solving abilities, a collaborative mindset, and resilience and adaptability. By developing and honing these competencies, students aspiring to become educational leaders can make a significant impact in shaping the future of education and positively influencing the lives of students, educators, and communities they serve.

Chapter 3: Navigating the Education System

Understanding the Structure of the Education System

As students, it is crucial to have a clear understanding of the structure of the education system. This knowledge will empower you to navigate through the complexities of educational leadership and policy, allowing you to make informed decisions about your academic journey.

The education system is composed of various levels, each with its unique purpose and objectives. At the primary level, students typically begin their education journey in kindergarten or elementary school. Here, the focus is on developing foundational skills, such as reading, writing, and basic math.

Moving up the ladder, the secondary level encompasses middle school and high school. During this phase, students delve deeper into subject areas and explore a wider range of disciplines. It is also at this stage that students start to consider their future career paths and make decisions regarding their academic trajectory.

Beyond high school, students have the option to pursue higher education, which includes colleges and universities. Higher education institutions offer undergraduate and graduate programs, allowing students to specialize in specific fields of study. This level of education is often seen as a pathway to acquiring advanced knowledge and skills, and it plays a significant role in shaping future leaders in various disciplines.

The structure of the education system is not limited to these levels alone; it also includes the administrative bodies and policies that govern education. Educational leadership and policy refer to the individuals and organizations responsible for making decisions regarding curriculum, assessment methods, funding, and overall educational standards.

Understanding the structure of the education system is essential for students interested in educational leadership and policy. By comprehending how decisions are made and how policies are implemented, students can actively engage in discussions and advocate for changes that will benefit themselves and their peers.

Moreover, having a grasp of the education system's structure allows students to make informed choices when selecting courses, schools, or even future careers. Recognizing the different levels and their objectives enables students to align their educational goals with the appropriate institutions or programs.

In conclusion, understanding the structure of the education system is vital for students interested in educational leadership and policy. By familiarizing themselves with the various levels and administrative bodies, students can actively participate in shaping their academic journeys and advocating for positive changes within the system. This knowledge empowers students to make informed decisions and align their educational goals with the appropriate paths, ultimately leading to success in their chosen fields.

Roles and Responsibilities of Education Stakeholders

In the complex and ever-evolving landscape of education, there are numerous stakeholders who play crucial roles in shaping educational policies and practices. Understanding the roles and responsibilities of these stakeholders is essential for students who are interested in educational leadership and policy. This subchapter will provide an overview of the key education stakeholders and their contributions to the education system.

1.   Students: As the primary beneficiaries of education, students have a responsibility to actively engage in their own learning. They should take ownership of their education by being proactive learners, participating in classroom discussions, asking questions, and seeking additional support when needed. Students also have the responsibility to provide feedback to their teachers and administrators to improve the quality of education.

2.   Teachers: Teachers are at the heart of the education system. They have the responsibility to create a positive and inclusive learning environment, design effective lesson plans, and deliver high-quality instruction. Additionally, teachers must assess student progress, provide timely and constructive feedback, and support students' social-emotional development. Teachers also have a responsibility to engage in professional development to continuously improve their teaching practices.

3.   Parents   and   Guardians: Parents and guardians play a crucial role in supporting their children's education. They have the responsibility to create a supportive home

environment that values education and promotes learning. Additionally, parents should communicate regularly with teachers, attend parent-teacher conferences, and collaborate with educators to support their child's academic and personal growth.

4. School Administrators: School administrators, including principals and district-level leaders, have the responsibility to develop and implement effective educational policies and strategies. They must oversee the daily operations of the school, ensure a safe and inclusive learning environment, and support teachers in their professional growth. Administrators also have the responsibility to engage with parents, community members, and other stakeholders to build strong partnerships.

5. Policy Makers: Policy makers at the local, state, and national levels have the responsibility to create and implement educational policies that promote equity and excellence. They must gather input from various stakeholders, including students, parents, teachers, and administrators, to develop evidence-based policies. Policy makers also have the responsibility to allocate resources effectively, address educational disparities, and advocate for the needs of all students.

Understanding the roles and responsibilities of education stakeholders is essential for students interested in educational leadership and policy. By recognizing the contributions of each stakeholder, students can gain a comprehensive understanding of the education system and contribute meaningfully to its improvement.

Key Decision-Making Processes in Education

In the complex and ever-evolving field of education, key decision-making processes play a crucial role in shaping policies and practices that impact students and the educational system as a whole. Understanding these processes is essential for students interested in educational leadership and policy, as it provides a foundation for meaningful change and improvement within the education system.

One of the key decision-making processes in education is curriculum development. Curriculum refers to the content, skills, and knowledge that students are expected to learn and the methods used to teach them. This process involves a careful analysis of educational goals, research on best practices, and collaboration among educators, policymakers, and other stakeholders. By participating in curriculum development, students can contribute to shaping the content and structure of their own education, ensuring that it is relevant, engaging, and aligned with their needs and aspirations.

Another critical decision-making process is the allocation of resources. Education requires the allocation of financial, human, and material resources to provide students with a quality learning experience. This process involves balancing competing needs and priorities, such as funding for classrooms, technology, professional development, and support services. Students interested in educational leadership and policy can advocate for equitable resource distribution, ensuring that all schools and students have access to the necessary tools and opportunities for success.

Additionally, decision-making processes in education encompass policies related to student assessment and evaluation. These policies determine how students' progress is measured, whether through standardized tests, project-based assessments, or other means. Understanding these processes is crucial for students as they navigate their educational journey, as it allows them to advocate for fair and comprehensive assessment methods that accurately reflect their abilities and growth.

Lastly, decision-making processes in education involve policies related to school governance and leadership. These policies determine how schools are managed and led, including the selection and evaluation of administrators, the involvement of parents and community members, and the establishment of a safe and inclusive learning environment. Students interested in educational leadership and policy can explore ways to enhance transparency, accountability, and collaboration within their schools, fostering a positive and empowering educational experience for all.

Overall, understanding the key decision-making processes in education is fundamental for students interested in educational leadership and policy. By actively participating in these processes, students can contribute to shaping their own education and the broader education system, making a lasting impact on the quality and equity of education for all.

Chapter 4: Education Policies and Their Impact

Introduction to Education Policies

Education is a fundamental aspect of society that shapes the future of individuals and communities. In order to ensure a high-quality education system, governments and institutions develop and implement education policies that guide the planning, organization, and delivery of educational programs. These policies are crucial as they impact various aspects of the education system, including curriculum development, teacher training, assessment, and funding.

The subchapter "Introduction to Education Policies" aims to provide students with a comprehensive understanding of the importance and impact of education policies in their lives as learners. By delving into this topic, students can gain insights into how policies shape their educational experiences and how they can contribute to shaping policies in the future.

One of the primary goals of education policies is to promote equity and access to education. Policies are designed to ensure that every student, regardless of their background or circumstances, has equal opportunities to receive a quality education. Students will learn about the various initiatives and strategies implemented to bridge educational gaps and promote inclusivity within the system.

Furthermore, education policies also govern the curriculum, which outlines the knowledge and skills students are expected to acquire. Students will explore how policies influence the creation and revision of the curriculum, as well as the importance of aligning it with societal needs and future career prospects. They will also gain an understanding of the role of standardized tests and assessments in evaluating student progress and informing policy decisions.

Another crucial aspect covered in this subchapter is teacher training and professional development. Education policies play a key role in establishing the qualifications and standards required for teachers. Students will learn about the importance of effective teacher training programs and ongoing professional development to ensure educators are equipped with the necessary skills to provide high-quality instruction.

Lastly, students will be introduced to the concept of educational funding and its role in policy implementation. They will explore different funding models and the allocation of resources to support various educational initiatives. Understanding the complexities of funding can help students comprehend the challenges faced by policymakers in ensuring adequate resources for schools and students.

By studying the subchapter "Introduction to Education Policies," students interested in educational leadership and policy will gain a deeper understanding of how policies shape their educational journey. Armed with this knowledge, students can actively engage in discussions and contribute to the development of effective education policies that promote equity, access, and excellence for all learners.

Analyzing the Impact of Policies on Students

In today's rapidly evolving education landscape, policies play a significant role in shaping the experiences of students. From curriculum standards to funding allocations, educational policies have a direct impact on the quality of education received by students. Therefore, it is crucial for students to understand and analyze these policies to advocate for their needs and ensure a successful educational journey.

This subchapter aims to provide students with the knowledge and tools necessary to critically examine the impact of policies on their education. By understanding the intricacies of educational leadership and policy, students can actively participate in shaping their own learning environment.

One of the key areas of focus will be curriculum standards. Students often encounter standardized testing and prescribed curricula that may not align with their unique learning styles or interests. By analyzing these policies, students can identify areas of improvement and propose alternative approaches that better cater to their needs. It is essential for students to understand the rationale behind curriculum decisions and the potential consequences for their educational development.

Furthermore, this subchapter will explore the impact of funding allocations on students. Educational policies often determine how resources are distributed among schools, which can result in disparities in access to essential materials, technology, and extracurricular activities. By analyzing funding policies, students can advocate for equitable resource allocation and work towards creating a level playing field for all learners.

Additionally, the subchapter will delve into policies related to student rights and wellbeing. Issues such as bullying prevention, mental health support, and inclusive education are vital in creating a safe and nurturing learning environment. Students must understand their rights and the policies in place to protect them, enabling them to actively participate in advocating for their own wellbeing.

Throughout this subchapter, students will learn how to analyze policies using critical thinking skills. They will explore the historical context, stakeholder perspectives, and potential unintended consequences of these policies. Students will also be encouraged to engage in open discussions, share their experiences, and propose alternative solutions that address their specific needs.

Ultimately, by analyzing the impact of policies on students, this subchapter empowers students to become informed and active participants in the educational decision-making process. By understanding the intricate relationship between educational leadership, policy, and their own experiences, students can advocate for positive change and contribute to a more inclusive and equitable education system.

Examining Policy Implementation Challenges

In the dynamic landscape of education, policies play a vital role in shaping the educational system. However, the successful implementation of these policies is often riddled with challenges. As students, it is essential to understand these challenges to navigate the education system effectively. This subchapter delves into the intricacies of policy implementation challenges in the context of educational leadership and policy.

One of the fundamental challenges in policy implementation is the gap between policy design and its execution. Educational policies are often crafted by policymakers who may not have a thorough understanding of the ground realities and complexities faced by students and educators. As a result, policies may lack practicality and fail to address the real needs of the education system. It is crucial for students to recognize this gap and advocate for policies that are grounded in reality.

Another challenge lies in the resistance to change from various stakeholders. Educational institutions, teachers, parents, and students themselves may resist policy changes due to a fear of the unknown or a perceived threat to their interests. This resistance can hinder the successful implementation of progressive policies. Students need to be proactive in understanding the rationale behind policy changes and engaging in constructive dialogue with stakeholders to address their concerns.

The limited resources available in the education system pose yet another challenge to policy implementation. Insufficient funding, outdated infrastructure, and a shortage of qualified teachers can hinder the execution of even the most well-intentioned policies.

Students must advocate for adequate resources to ensure policies are implemented effectively and equitably.

Furthermore, the lack of effective communication and coordination between policymakers and implementers can impede policy implementation. Clear communication channels, feedback mechanisms, and collaboration among all stakeholders are essential to ensure policies are understood and executed correctly. Students should actively participate in discussions and engage in platforms where they can voice their concerns and contribute to policy dialogue.

Lastly, the ever-changing political landscape can pose challenges to policy implementation. Educational policies may be subject to shifts in government priorities and ideologies, leading to inconsistent implementation and uncertainty. Students must remain informed about the political context and engage in advocacy efforts to maintain continuity in policy implementation.

Navigating the challenges of policy implementation in educational leadership and policy is a crucial skill for students. By understanding the gap between policy design and execution, addressing resistance to change, advocating for resources, fostering communication and coordination, and staying informed about the political landscape, students can actively contribute to the improvement of the education system. This subchapter equips students with the knowledge and tools needed to navigate these challenges and become effective agents of change in the realm of educational leadership and policy.

Chapter 5: Student Advocacy and Leadership

Empowering Students to Become Advocates

In today's rapidly changing world, students have a crucial role to play in shaping educational leadership and policy. As young individuals who directly experience the education system, students have unique insights and perspectives that can drive positive change. This subchapter aims to equip students with the knowledge, skills, and tools to become advocates for their own education and the education of others.

Understanding the importance of advocacy is the first step for students. By advocating for their needs, concerns, and aspirations, students can influence decision-makers and drive meaningful reforms. This subchapter will explore various aspects of educational advocacy, including its definition, different forms, and its impact on policy-making processes.

Advocacy is not limited to protests and demonstrations; it encompasses a wide range of activities that aim to bring about change. From writing persuasive letters to policymakers, organizing student-led initiatives, participating in school board meetings, or even utilizing social media platforms, students have numerous avenues to advocate for their rights and educational improvement. This subchapter will provide practical tips and guidance on how students can effectively carry out these advocacy activities.

Moreover, understanding educational leadership and policy is essential for effective advocacy. Students must have knowledge of how educational systems operate, the role of policymakers, and the decision-making processes involved in shaping educational policies.

This subchapter will delve into these topics, offering insights into the complexities of educational leadership and policy and providing students with the necessary background to navigate the system.

Additionally, this subchapter will highlight successful student-led advocacy movements and initiatives from around the world. By showcasing inspiring stories of young activists who have made a difference in their communities, students will be motivated and empowered to take action themselves. These stories will demonstrate that age is not a barrier to effecting change and that students have the power to shape their own educational experiences.

Ultimately, by empowering students to become advocates, this subchapter aims to foster a sense of agency and responsibility among students. It encourages them to take an active role in shaping their education and creating a positive impact within the educational system. Through advocacy, students can amplify their voices, address their concerns, and contribute to the development of inclusive and student-centered educational policies.

Developing Leadership Skills in Education

In today's rapidly changing educational landscape, leadership skills are more important than ever. As students, you have the power to shape the future of education and make a positive impact on your peers, schools, and communities. This subchapter will explore the importance of developing leadership skills in education and provide practical strategies for honing these skills.

Leadership skills are not limited to those in formal leadership positions such as principals or superintendents. Every student has the potential to be a leader within their own academic journey. By developing leadership skills, you can become a proactive agent of change, advocate for educational policies, and inspire others to reach their full potential.

One crucial aspect of developing leadership skills in education is self-awareness. Understanding your strengths, weaknesses, and values will help you navigate the educational system effectively. Reflect on your interests and passions, and consider how they align with educational leadership and policy. This self-reflection will guide you in choosing the areas of education where you can make the greatest impact.

Effective communication is another vital leadership skill. As a student leader, you must be able to articulate your ideas, concerns, and goals clearly and persuasively. This subchapter will provide practical tips for improving your communication skills, including active listening, public speaking, and effective writing.

Collaboration and teamwork are also essential in educational leadership. As a student, you will often work with other students, teachers, administrators, and community members to bring about positive change. Learning to work collaboratively, respect diverse perspectives, and build consensus will enhance your leadership skills and increase your effectiveness in creating meaningful educational reforms.

Additionally, this subchapter will explore the importance of critical thinking and problem-solving in educational leadership. As a student leader, you will encounter complex challenges and conflicting viewpoints. Developing strong critical thinking skills will enable you to analyze problems, evaluate evidence, and make informed decisions.

Finally, this subchapter will address the importance of resilience and adaptability in educational leadership. The educational landscape is constantly evolving, and successful leaders must be able to navigate these changes with resilience and flexibility. By developing a growth mindset and embracing challenges, you can become a resilient leader who inspires others to overcome obstacles and achieve their goals.

In conclusion, developing leadership skills in education is crucial for students who aspire to make a positive impact on the educational system. By cultivating self-awareness, communication skills, collaboration, critical thinking, and resilience, you can become an effective student leader who advocates for change and influences educational policies. This subchapter will provide you with practical strategies and insights to help you navigate the complex world of educational leadership and policy.

Strategies for Effectively Communicating with Education Authorities

Communicating with education authorities, such as school administrators, policymakers, and educational leaders, can be essential for students who want to make their voices heard and contribute to shaping the education system. Effective communication is crucial in advocating for change, addressing concerns, and promoting policies that benefit students. In this subchapter, we will explore some strategies that students can use to effectively communicate with education authorities.

1. Be Informed: Before engaging with education authorities, it is important to gather relevant information about the educational policies, regulations, and initiatives that affect your school or district. Stay updated on current trends, research, and best practices in educational leadership and policy. This knowledge will help you articulate your ideas and arguments effectively.

2. Build Relationships: Establishing positive relationships with education authorities is vital for effective communication. Attend school board meetings, join student councils, and engage in extracurricular activities that involve educational leadership and policy. By interacting with education authorities regularly, you can gain their trust and be seen as a credible and reliable source of information.

3. Develop Clear and Concise Messages: When communicating with education authorities, it is crucial to present your ideas or concerns in a clear and concise manner. Develop well-structured arguments, supported by evidence and examples. Use language that is easy to understand and avoid jargon that may confuse or alienate your audience.

4. Utilize Different Communication Channels: Education authorities receive numerous communications on a daily basis. To increase your chances of being heard, utilize various communication channels such as emails, letters, social media, and in-person meetings. Each channel has its own advantages, so choose the one that best suits your message and target audience.

5. Collaborate with Peers: Collective action is often more impactful than individual efforts. Collaborate with fellow students who share similar concerns or goals. Form student organizations or advocacy groups to amplify your voices and increase your influence. By working together, you can achieve more significant changes in educational leadership and policy.

6. Maintain Professionalism and Respect: When communicating with education authorities, always maintain a professional and respectful tone. Even if you disagree with their decisions, it is important to express your opinions in a courteous manner. Remember that respectful dialogue can lead to better understanding and more productive outcomes.

By implementing these strategies, students interested in educational leadership and policy can effectively communicate with education authorities and become active contributors in shaping the education system. Remember, your voice matters, and by engaging with education authorities, you can make a meaningful difference in your educational journey and those of future students.

Chapter 6: Educational Policy Development

The Process of Policy Development

As students, it is important to understand the process of policy development within the education system. Policies play a crucial role in shaping the educational landscape and addressing various issues and concerns that arise within schools and districts. This subchapter will provide an overview of the policy development process, empowering students with the knowledge to navigate the education system more effectively.

Policy development begins with the identification of a problem or a need for change within the education system. This could range from addressing achievement gaps to improving school safety or enhancing curriculum standards. Once the problem is identified, policymakers and stakeholders collaborate to develop potential solutions.

The next step involves conducting extensive research and gathering data to support the proposed policy changes. This may include analyzing academic research, conducting surveys, or consulting with experts in the field. Data-driven policies are more likely to be effective and have a positive impact on students and schools.

After the research phase, policymakers draft the policy, outlining its objectives, strategies, and potential implementation challenges. It is crucial for students to familiarize themselves with the language and key components of policy documents, as these policies directly affect their educational experiences.

Once the policy is drafted, it goes through a review and revision process. This involves seeking feedback and input from various stakeholders such as teachers, administrators, parents, and students themselves. Students can actively engage in this process by participating in public hearings, providing written feedback, or joining student-led advocacy groups.

After revisions, the policy moves into the implementation phase. This requires collaboration between policymakers, administrators, and educators to ensure that the policy is effectively put into practice. Students can play an active role in this phase by monitoring the implementation, providing feedback, and voicing their concerns if they perceive any issues or challenges.

Finally, policies undergo evaluation to assess their effectiveness. This involves measuring outcomes and determining whether the policy has achieved its intended objectives. Students should be aware of the evaluation process and, if necessary, advocate for adjustments or improvements based on their experiences and perspectives.

Understanding the process of policy development empowers students to engage in meaningful discussions, advocate for their needs, and actively participate in shaping educational policies. By being informed and actively involved, students can contribute to creating a more inclusive and effective education system that meets the needs of all learners.

Identifying and Addressing Education System Issues

In today's rapidly evolving world, the education system plays a crucial role in shaping the future of individuals and societies. However, it is not without its flaws and challenges. To truly understand and navigate the education system, students must be aware of the issues that exist within it and how they can actively address them. This subchapter aims to shed light on some of these issues and provide students with valuable insights into the realm of educational leadership and policy.

One prominent issue in the education system is the lack of equal access to quality education. Socioeconomic disparities, geographic location, and systemic biases can all contribute to unequal opportunities for students. As students, it is important to recognize these disparities and advocate for equitable education for all. This may involve supporting initiatives that provide resources and support to underprivileged communities, or raising awareness about the importance of inclusive and diverse educational environments.

Another critical issue is the prevalence of standardized testing. While assessments are necessary to measure academic progress, an overemphasis on standardized tests can hinder creativity, critical thinking, and holistic education. Students can address this issue by exploring alternative assessment methods, promoting project-based learning, and advocating for a more comprehensive evaluation of academic achievements.

Furthermore, the education system often fails to adapt to the rapid changes in the job market and technological advancements. Many students find themselves ill-prepared for the demands of the 21st-century workforce. By engaging in conversations about curriculum development and participating in student-led initiatives, students can influence educational policies to better align with the skills and knowledge necessary for future success.

Lastly, the mental health and well-being of students are increasingly becoming areas of concern within the education system. Pressures from academic expectations, social dynamics, and extracurricular commitments can take a toll on students' mental health. It is crucial for students to advocate for comprehensive mental health support and resources within their educational institutions, fostering a nurturing environment that prioritizes well-being alongside academic achievement.

By identifying and addressing these education system issues, students can play an active role in shaping the future of education. This subchapter aims to empower students to navigate the complexities of educational leadership and policy, encouraging them to become agents of positive change within their educational communities. By understanding the issues and taking action, students can contribute to a more inclusive, equitable, and effective education system that prepares individuals for the challenges and opportunities of the future.

Engaging Students in Policy Discussions and Decision-Making

As students, we often find ourselves on the receiving end of educational policies and decisions made by administrators and policymakers. However, it is crucial for us to recognize that we have a voice and can actively participate in policy discussions and decision-making processes. By engaging in these discussions, we can shape the policies that directly impact our education and make a positive difference in our schools and communities.

Policy discussions and decision-making are essential components of educational leadership and policy. These processes involve analyzing and addressing various issues, such as curriculum development, school funding, and student support services. Engaging in these discussions allows us to share our perspectives, experiences, and concerns, ensuring that policies are inclusive and meet the needs of all students.

One way to get involved in policy discussions is by joining student organizations or clubs that focus on educational leadership and policy. These groups offer a platform for students to come together, discuss relevant issues, and advocate for change. By participating in these organizations, we can collaborate with like-minded individuals, learn about policy-making processes, and develop leadership skills.

Additionally, attending school board meetings and public forums is an excellent opportunity to engage in policy discussions. These events provide a platform for students to voice their opinions, ask questions, and offer suggestions. By actively participating in these meetings, we can demonstrate our commitment to creating a positive educational environment and influence decision-makers.

Furthermore, utilizing digital platforms and social media can amplify our voices and reach a broader audience. Sharing our thoughts and experiences on educational policies through blog posts, videos, or social media campaigns can spark conversations and generate awareness. It is important to provide evidence-based arguments and propose practical solutions to ensure our voices are taken seriously.

Lastly, building relationships with teachers, administrators, and policymakers can enhance our influence in policy discussions. By cultivating these relationships, we can establish trust and open lines of communication. Sharing our concerns and ideas directly with decision-makers can lead to meaningful changes in policies that affect us.

Engaging in policy discussions and decision-making empowers us as students to actively shape our educational experiences. By participating in student organizations, attending meetings, utilizing digital platforms, and building relationships, we can contribute to creating policies that promote equity, inclusivity, and excellence in education. Together, let us make our voices heard and navigate the education system towards a brighter future.

Chapter 7: Addressing Educational Inequalities

Understanding Educational Inequalities

In today's diverse and rapidly changing educational landscape, it is crucial for students to have a deep understanding of the concept of educational inequalities. This subchapter aims to shed light on this critical issue, providing students with valuable insights into the factors that contribute to these disparities, their consequences, and potential solutions.

Educational inequalities refer to the unequal distribution of educational resources and opportunities among students, often resulting in disparities in academic achievement and outcomes. These disparities can arise from various factors, including socioeconomic status, race, ethnicity, gender, geographic location, and disability. Understanding the root causes of these inequalities is essential for students interested in educational leadership and policy, as it is the first step towards creating a more equitable and inclusive education system.

One key factor contributing to educational inequalities is socioeconomic status. Research consistently shows that students from low-income backgrounds face numerous barriers to educational success. These barriers may include limited access to quality schools, inadequate resources, lack of parental involvement, and increased exposure to adverse childhood experiences. Students aspiring to leadership roles in education must recognize the impact of socioeconomic status on educational opportunities and work towards implementing policies that level the playing field for all students.

Moreover, racial and ethnic disparities in education persist, highlighting the need for a comprehensive understanding of these inequalities. Students from marginalized racial and ethnic backgrounds often face discrimination, cultural biases, and limited access to educational resources. By examining these disparities, students can develop strategies to promote inclusivity, cultural sensitivity, and diversity within the education system.

Gender also plays a significant role in educational inequalities. Historically, girls have faced barriers to education, but progress has been made in recent years. However, gender disparities still exist, particularly in certain fields such as STEM (science, technology, engineering, and mathematics). Students interested in educational leadership and policy must be aware of these gender disparities and work towards creating an inclusive environment where all students have equal access to educational opportunities, regardless of their gender.

Geographic location is another factor contributing to educational inequalities. Rural areas often lack the same resources and opportunities available in urban or suburban regions. Students interested in educational leadership and policy must understand the unique challenges faced by rural schools and work towards bridging the gap between rural and urban education.

Lastly, students with disabilities face significant educational disparities. Inclusive education policies and practices are crucial to ensure that students with disabilities receive the necessary support and accommodations to succeed academically.

By understanding the various factors that contribute to educational inequalities, students interested in educational leadership and policy can become advocates for change. They can work towards creating policies that address these disparities and promote equitable access to quality education for all students, regardless of their background. Through their efforts, they can contribute to building a more just and inclusive education system that empowers every student to reach their full potential.

Examining the Role of Educational Leadership in Addressing Inequalities

In today's society, educational leadership plays a critical role in addressing inequalities within the education system. Educational leaders are responsible for shaping policies and practices that promote equity and ensure that every student has access to quality education, regardless of their background or circumstances. Understanding the role of educational leadership in addressing inequalities is essential for students who are interested in pursuing careers in educational leadership and policy.

One of the primary functions of educational leaders is to advocate for educational equity. They are responsible for identifying and addressing disparities in educational opportunities, resources, and outcomes among different student populations. By examining data, conducting research, and engaging with various stakeholders, educational leaders can identify systemic barriers and develop strategies to overcome them. These strategies may include implementing inclusive policies, providing targeted support to disadvantaged students, and fostering a culture of diversity and inclusion within schools.

Educational leaders also play a crucial role in promoting social justice within the education system. They are responsible for creating environments that respect and celebrate diversity, where all students feel valued and included. This involves addressing issues of discrimination, bias, and prejudice that may exist within schools and working towards creating a more inclusive and equitable educational experience for all students.

Furthermore, educational leaders are instrumental in ensuring that all students have access to high-quality educational opportunities. They are responsible for developing and implementing curriculum and instructional practices that meet the needs of diverse learners. This may involve providing additional resources and support to students who are academically disadvantaged, promoting culturally responsive teaching practices, and creating opportunities for student voice and agency.

In conclusion, educational leadership plays a vital role in addressing inequalities within the education system. Educational leaders have the power and responsibility to advocate for equity, promote social justice, and ensure that all students have access to high-quality education. By understanding the role of educational leadership in addressing inequalities, students interested in educational leadership and policy can contribute to creating a more equitable and inclusive education system for all.

Advocating for Equity in Education

In the pursuit of creating a fair and just education system, advocating for equity in education is of paramount importance. As students, it is essential for us to understand the significance of educational leadership and policy in ensuring that every individual has equal access to quality education, regardless of their background or circumstances. This subchapter aims to shed light on the importance of advocating for equity in education and the role that students can play in this endeavor.

Equity in education refers to the principle of fairness, where every student has the opportunity to succeed and reach their full potential. Unfortunately, our education system often fails to provide equal opportunities for all students, especially those from marginalized communities. Educational leadership and policy are crucial in addressing these disparities and implementing strategies to level the playing field.

Advocacy is the key to bringing about change in any system, and education is no exception. As students, we have a unique perspective and firsthand experience of the challenges and barriers we face in our educational journey. Through our voices, we can advocate for policies and practices that promote equity, diversity, and inclusion in education.

One of the most effective ways to advocate for equity in education is by engaging with educational leaders and policymakers. By actively participating in school boards, student unions, or student councils, we can voice our concerns and propose changes that promote a more equitable system. Additionally, we can collaborate with like-minded individuals and organizations to raise awareness, organize events, and initiate campaigns to address specific issues related to equity in education.

Moreover, it is crucial to educate ourselves about the existing policies and legislation that impact education. By understanding the intricacies of these policies, we can identify areas that need improvement and advocate for necessary changes. We can also leverage social media platforms to share our experiences and ideas, amplifying our voices and reaching a broader audience.

Advocating for equity in education is not a task that can be accomplished overnight. It requires persistence, determination, and collaboration. However, as students with a vested interest in our education, we have the power to drive change and make a difference. By advocating for equity in education, we can contribute to the creation of a more just and inclusive education system that benefits all students, regardless of their background or circumstances.

In conclusion, advocating for equity in education is a crucial aspect of educational leadership and policy. As students, we must recognize the importance of our voices and actively engage in advocating for change. By participating in decision-making processes, educating ourselves, and collaborating with others, we can work towards creating a more equitable education system. Together, we can pave the way for a brighter future where every student has an equal opportunity to thrive and succeed.

Chapter 8: Promoting Student Well-being and Mental Health

Recognizing the Importance of Student Well-being

In today's fast-paced and demanding educational landscape, it is crucial for students to recognize the importance of their well-being. As students, we often find ourselves juggling numerous responsibilities, from academic commitments to extracurricular activities and personal relationships. However, amidst this whirlwind of obligations, it is essential to prioritize and nurture our well-being.

Student well-being encompasses not only our physical health but also our mental, emotional, and social well-being. It is the harmonious balance of these aspects that enables us to thrive academically, socially, and personally. In this subchapter, we will explore why recognizing and prioritizing our well-being is essential for success in educational leadership and policy.

Firstly, our well-being impacts our academic performance. When we are physically and mentally healthy, we can concentrate better, retain information effectively, and perform at our best. By taking care of ourselves, we enhance our ability to learn, solve problems, and engage in critical thinking. Moreover, a positive state of mind allows us to approach challenges with resilience and perseverance.

Secondly, student well-being plays a significant role in our overall personal development. When we prioritize our well-being, we cultivate self-awareness, emotional intelligence, and mindfulness. These qualities are invaluable in educational leadership and policy as they enable us to understand and empathize with the needs of our peers, teachers, and administrators. Additionally, a healthy sense of self contributes to effective communication, collaboration, and conflict resolution – crucial skills in the realm of educational leadership.

Furthermore, recognizing the importance of student well-being fosters a positive school culture. As students, we are not only recipients of education but also active participants in the educational system. By prioritizing our well-being, we set an example for our peers and contribute to creating a supportive and compassionate learning environment. When students are happy, healthy, and engaged, it positively impacts the entire school community and enhances the educational experience for everyone involved.

In conclusion, recognizing and prioritizing student well-being is of utmost importance in educational leadership and policy. By taking care of ourselves physically, mentally, and emotionally, we enhance our academic performance, personal development, and contribute to a positive school culture. As students, let us embrace the significance of our well-being and make it a priority in our educational journey.

Understanding the Impact of Educational Policies on Mental Health

In recent years, the importance of mental health in educational settings has gained significant attention. As students, it is crucial for us to understand how educational policies can have a profound impact on our mental well-being. This subchapter aims to explore the intricate relationship between educational policies and mental health, shedding light on the potential challenges and opportunities that arise within the realm of educational leadership and policy.

Educational policies play a pivotal role in shaping the learning environment, curriculum, and overall student experience. However, it is essential to recognize that these policies have a direct and indirect impact on our mental health. For instance, policies that prioritize high-stakes testing and academic competition can create immense stress and anxiety among students. The pressure to perform well can lead to burnout, decreased self-esteem, and even the development of mental health disorders.

On the other hand, educational policies that emphasize holistic well-being, support systems, and mental health awareness can contribute to a positive and nurturing learning environment. These policies aim to create a culture of care and understanding, acknowledging the unique challenges students face in their academic journey. By promoting mental health resources, counseling services, and stress-reducing strategies, educational policies can empower students to prioritize their well-being while pursuing their educational goals.

Navigating the education system requires an awareness of the policies that shape our educational experience and an understanding of their potential impact on our mental health. By advocating for inclusive policies that address mental health, we can contribute to a system that prioritizes the overall well-being of students and fosters a positive learning environment.

Furthermore, as students interested in educational leadership and policy, it is essential to engage in conversations surrounding mental health advocacy. By actively participating in discussions, research, and initiatives, we can influence the development and implementation of policies that promote mental health and well-being. By amplifying our voices and sharing our experiences, we can contribute to a more compassionate and student-centered education system.

In conclusion, the impact of educational policies on mental health is a critical aspect to consider in our educational journey. By understanding the potential challenges and opportunities that arise in the realm of educational leadership and policy, we can actively work towards creating a system that prioritizes the mental well-being of students. As students interested in educational leadership and policy, we have the power to shape the future of education and advocate for policies that foster a positive and supportive learning environment.

Strategies for Promoting Student Well-being in Education

As students, we understand the importance of a healthy and supportive learning environment. Our well-being plays a crucial role in our educational journey, shaping not only our academic success but also our personal growth. In this subchapter, we will explore various strategies for promoting student well-being in education, focusing on the niches of educational leadership and policy.

1. Implementing Comprehensive Mental Health Support: Educational leaders and policymakers should prioritize the implementation of comprehensive mental health support systems within schools and universities. This includes the provision of counseling services, access to mental health professionals, and the promotion of mental health awareness campaigns. By destigmatizing mental health issues and providing adequate support, students can thrive academically and personally.

2. Encouraging Physical Activity and Healthy Lifestyles: Educational leaders can promote student well-being by encouraging physical activity and healthy lifestyles. This can be achieved through the integration of physical education classes, sports teams, and extracurricular activities that promote active living. Policies can also be put in place to ensure access to nutritious meals within schools and universities.

3. Fostering a Sense of Belonging and Inclusivity: Students thrive in environments where they feel a sense of belonging and inclusivity. Educational leaders should prioritize creating safe spaces that celebrate diversity and respect individual identities. Policies that address bullying, discrimination, and harassment can help foster a supportive environment where students can flourish.

4. Promoting Student Agency and Voice: Encouraging student agency and giving them a voice in decision-making processes can greatly enhance their well-being. Educational leaders and policymakers should create opportunities for students to participate in school governance, allowing them to have a say in matters that directly affect them. This fosters a sense of empowerment and ownership over their educational experience.

5. Providing Adequate Academic Support: Academic challenges can significantly impact student well-being. Educational leaders should ensure that students have access to tutors, academic resources, and support services to help them succeed. Policies can be implemented to address workload management, exam stress, and the promotion of healthy study habits.

In conclusion, promoting student well-being in education requires a multi-faceted approach that considers various aspects of their lives. By implementing strategies such as comprehensive mental health support, fostering inclusivity, and providing academic support, educational leaders and policymakers can create a nurturing environment that supports students' overall well-being. As students, it is essential for us to advocate for our well-being and actively engage with educational leadership and policy to create positive change in our educational institutions.

Chapter 9: The Future of Educational Leadership and Policy

Emerging Trends in Educational Leadership

In today's rapidly changing education landscape, it is crucial for students to understand the emerging trends in educational leadership and policy. These trends shape the way educational institutions are run and have a direct impact on the quality of education students receive. By being aware of these trends, students can better navigate the education system and make informed decisions about their own educational journey.

One of the key emerging trends in educational leadership is a shift towards student-centered learning. In the past, education was often seen as a one-size-fits-all approach, with teachers delivering information and students passively absorbing it. However, research has shown that students learn best when they are actively engaged in the learning process. Educational leaders are now focusing on creating learning environments that empower students to take ownership of their education, encouraging critical thinking, problem-solving, and collaboration.

Another important trend is the integration of technology in education. With advancements in technology, educational leaders are leveraging digital tools to enhance the learning experience. This includes the use of online platforms, interactive learning materials, and virtual reality simulations. Technology not only makes learning more engaging and interactive but also allows for personalized learning experiences tailored to each student's needs and abilities.

In recent years, there has also been a growing emphasis on diversity, equity, and inclusion in educational leadership. Educational leaders are recognizing the importance of creating inclusive environments that celebrate and respect students from diverse backgrounds. This includes addressing systemic barriers to education, promoting culturally responsive teaching practices, and fostering a sense of belonging for all students. By embracing diversity, educational leaders aim to create a more equitable education system where every student has an equal opportunity to succeed.

Lastly, the field of educational leadership is witnessing a shift towards data-driven decision-making. With the availability of vast amounts of data, educational leaders are using analytics to inform their decision-making processes. This includes analyzing student performance data, tracking attendance rates, and evaluating the effectiveness of different instructional methods. By using data to drive decision-making, educational leaders can identify areas for improvement and implement evidence-based strategies to enhance student outcomes.

In conclusion, understanding the emerging trends in educational leadership is essential for students interested in educational leadership and policy. By keeping abreast of these trends, students can actively participate in shaping the future of education and make informed choices about their educational journey. Whether it is the shift towards student-centered learning, the integration of technology, the focus on diversity and inclusion, or the use of data-driven decision-making, these trends are transforming the education system and creating new opportunities for students to thrive.

The Influence of Technology on Education Policies

In this rapidly evolving digital age, technology has become an integral part of our lives, significantly impacting various sectors, including education. The influence of technology on education policies is a topic of great importance for students studying educational leadership and policy. As future leaders in the field, it is crucial for students to understand the implications and benefits of technology integration in educational settings.

One of the most significant impacts of technology on education policies is the shift towards digital learning platforms. Traditional classroom settings are gradually being replaced by online learning platforms, virtual classrooms, and interactive educational tools. This change has been accelerated by the recent global pandemic, which forced educational institutions to adapt quickly to remote learning.

The integration of technology in education policies brings numerous advantages. Firstly, it provides students with access to a vast array of resources and information. With just a few clicks, students can access e-books, research articles, and multimedia materials, enhancing their learning experiences. Furthermore, technology enables personalized learning, allowing students to learn at their own pace and in their preferred style.

Additionally, technology integration in education policies promotes collaborative learning. Students can now participate in virtual group projects, engage in online discussions, and receive real-time feedback from their peers and instructors. This fosters critical thinking, problem-solving, and communication skills, which are essential in the 21st-century workforce.

However, challenges and concerns also arise with the increasing influence of technology on education policies. One major concern is the digital divide, where students from low-income backgrounds may not have equal access to technology and reliable internet connections. This issue highlights the need for policymakers to address the disparities in access to ensure equity in education.

Furthermore, there are concerns about the overreliance on technology, leading to reduced face-to-face interactions and social skills development. It is crucial for policymakers to strike a balance between technology integration and maintaining human connections within the educational environment.

In conclusion, the influence of technology on education policies is a transformative force shaping the future of educational leadership and policy. It brings numerous benefits such as access to resources, personalized learning, and collaborative opportunities. However, policymakers must also address concerns such as the digital divide and the potential impact on social skills development. As students studying educational leadership and policy, it is essential to critically analyze the influence of technology and advocate for policies that promote equitable and effective integration of technology in educational settings.

Envisioning a Student-Centered Education System

In today's rapidly changing world, the traditional education system is no longer sufficient to prepare students for the challenges they will face in their future careers and lives. As students, you are the primary stakeholders in the education system, and your needs and aspirations should be at the forefront of any educational policy or leadership decision-making. This subchapter explores the concept of a student-centered education system and its implications for both educational leadership and policy.

A student-centered education system places students' learning needs and interests at the core of every decision. It recognizes that students have unique talents, aspirations, and learning styles, and seeks to provide personalized learning experiences that cater to individual strengths and weaknesses. This approach moves away from the one-size-fits-all model and embraces the idea that education should be tailored to the diverse needs of each student.

Educational leadership plays a crucial role in envisioning and implementing a student-centered education system. Effective leaders understand the importance of involving students in the decision-making process, fostering a collaborative environment that values student input, and actively seeking feedback from students. They encourage student representation in school boards and committees, ensuring that students have a voice in shaping policies that directly impact their educational experience.

From a policy perspective, a student-centered education system requires a shift in focus from standardized testing and rote memorization towards holistic, skills-based assessments. It calls for policies that prioritize the development of critical thinking, problem-solving, creativity, and collaboration skills. These policies should also support the integration of technology in education, providing students with access to digital resources and facilitating innovative teaching methods.

Furthermore, a student-centered education system recognizes the importance of inclusive education and equity. It acknowledges that every student, regardless of their background or abilities, deserves equal opportunities to succeed. Policies should address the achievement gaps that exist among different student populations and ensure that resources are distributed fairly.

By envisioning and advocating for a student-centered education system, students can actively participate in shaping their own educational experiences. It empowers students to take ownership of their learning, encourages creativity and innovation, and prepares them for the complexities of the modern world. Ultimately, a student-centered education system has the potential to create a generation of lifelong learners who are well-equipped to navigate the challenges and opportunities that lie ahead.

As students interested in educational leadership and policy, it is crucial to understand the importance of a student-centered approach and actively engage in discussions and initiatives that promote its implementation. By advocating for a student-centered education system, you can contribute to creating positive changes in the education landscape and ensure that your voices are heard.

Chapter 10: Navigating Career Paths in Educational Leadership

Exploring Career Opportunities in Educational Leadership

For students interested in the field of educational leadership and policy, there is a wide range of career opportunities awaiting you. This subchapter aims to provide an overview of the various paths you can take within this field and highlight the importance of educational leadership in shaping the future of our schools and educational systems.

Educational leadership is a critical aspect of the education system, as it involves making decisions and implementing policies that directly impact students, teachers, and communities. It requires individuals who are passionate about education and have a strong desire to create positive change and improve learning outcomes.

One of the most common career paths in educational leadership is becoming a school administrator. School principals, assistant principals, and other administrative roles play a crucial role in managing day-to-day operations, fostering a positive learning environment, and ensuring that teachers and students have the necessary resources and support.

Another exciting career opportunity in educational leadership is working as an education policy analyst or researcher. These professionals analyze educational policies and their impact on various stakeholders, such as students, teachers, and parents. They conduct research to inform policy decisions, advocate for necessary changes, and evaluate the effectiveness of existing policies.

For those interested in working at a broader level, educational leadership roles in government agencies and non-profit organizations are also available. These positions involve developing and implementing policies at the state or national level, advocating for educational equity, and ensuring that all students have equal access to quality education.

Additionally, there is a growing demand for educational consultants and instructional coaches who provide guidance and support to teachers and administrators. These professionals work closely with educators to improve teaching strategies, curriculum development, and student engagement.

To pursue a career in educational leadership, it is essential to acquire the necessary qualifications and experience. Many universities offer graduate programs in educational leadership and policy, providing students with the knowledge and skills required for leadership roles. Additionally, gaining practical experience through internships, volunteer work, or part-time positions in educational settings can be invaluable in building a strong foundation for a career in this field.

In conclusion, exploring career opportunities in educational leadership can lead to fulfilling and impactful roles within the education system. Whether you choose to become a school administrator, policy analyst, consultant, or work in a government agency, the field of educational leadership offers diverse paths to make a positive difference in the lives of students and contribute to the improvement of our education system.

Building the Skills and Qualifications for Leadership Roles

In today's rapidly evolving educational landscape, the demand for effective leaders in educational institutions is higher than ever before. The ability to lead and navigate the complex world of educational leadership and policy requires a unique set of skills and qualifications. This subchapter aims to illuminate the path towards developing these essential attributes for students interested in pursuing leadership roles in education.

First and foremost, a solid foundation of academic knowledge is crucial for aspiring educational leaders. This encompasses a deep understanding of educational theories, policies, and practices. By immersing oneself in educational literature and staying abreast of the latest research and developments, students can acquire the necessary knowledge to effectively analyze and address the challenges faced by educational institutions.

However, leadership in education extends far beyond theoretical knowledge. Practical experience is equally important. Engaging in internships, volunteering, or part-time positions in educational settings allows students to gain hands-on experience and develop a comprehensive understanding of the intricacies of the field. By actively participating in school projects, extracurricular activities, or community initiatives, students can develop skills such as communication, problem-solving, critical thinking, and teamwork, which are vital for effective leadership.

Additionally, cultivating a strong network within the educational leadership and policy niches is crucial. Attending conferences, seminars, and workshops provide opportunities to connect with professionals in the field, exchange ideas, and gain insights into the latest trends and best practices. Building mentorships with experienced educational leaders can also be immensely valuable, as their guidance and support can help students navigate the complexities of leadership roles and provide them with valuable advice and opportunities.

Furthermore, a commitment to lifelong learning is essential for aspiring educational leaders. The field of education is constantly evolving, with new research, technologies, and policies shaping the landscape. By actively seeking out professional development opportunities, such as advanced degrees, certifications, or specialized training programs, students can enhance their knowledge and skills, keeping them at the forefront of the field.

In conclusion, building the skills and qualifications for leadership roles in educational leadership and policy requires a multifaceted approach. It involves a combination of academic knowledge, practical experience, networking, and a commitment to continuous learning. By investing in these areas, students can position themselves as competent and effective leaders capable of driving positive change in educational institutions.

Networking and Professional Development Opportunities

In today's rapidly changing world, it is essential for students pursuing a career in educational leadership and policy to understand the significance of networking and professional development opportunities. These opportunities not only enhance knowledge and skills but also open doors to new collaborations, innovative ideas, and career advancement. This subchapter will explore the importance of networking and provide guidance on how to maximize professional development opportunities in the field of educational leadership and policy.

Networking plays a pivotal role in the educational leadership and policy domain. Building connections with professionals, educators, and policymakers can provide invaluable insights into the current trends, challenges, and opportunities in the field. It offers a platform to exchange ideas, learn from experienced individuals, and create a network of support and collaboration. Attending conferences, workshops, and seminars related to educational leadership and policy can provide students with opportunities to meet influential figures and establish meaningful connections. Additionally, joining professional organizations and online communities can foster ongoing networking, discussions, and learning.

Professional development opportunities are essential for students in educational leadership and policy to stay updated with the latest research, best practices, and policies shaping the field. By actively participating in workshops, webinars, and training sessions, students can enhance their knowledge and skills in areas such as curriculum design, strategic planning, policy analysis, and leadership development. These opportunities also allow students to interact with experts in the field, engage in critical discussions, and gain practical insights into the challenges and complexities of educational leadership and policy.

To maximize networking and professional development opportunities, students should be proactive and strategic. They can start by identifying their goals and areas of interest within educational leadership and policy. By understanding their specific niche, students can tailor their networking efforts and professional development activities to align with their career aspirations. Students should actively seek out conferences, seminars, and workshops that focus on their areas of interest. They should also consider joining relevant professional organizations and online communities to connect with like-minded individuals and access resources that can contribute to their professional growth.

In conclusion, networking and professional development opportunities are crucial for students in the field of educational leadership and policy. By actively engaging in these opportunities, students can expand their knowledge, build meaningful connections, and gain practical insights into the field. By being proactive and strategic, students can maximize the benefits of networking and professional development, ultimately positioning themselves for success in their educational leadership and policy careers.

Chapter 11: Conclusion

Reflecting on the Journey of Navigating the Education System

As students, we often find ourselves navigating the complex landscape of the education system. From the moment we enter school to the day we graduate, we encounter various challenges and opportunities that shape our educational journey. In this subchapter, we will take a moment to reflect on this journey, exploring the highs and lows, and understanding the importance of educational leadership and policy in shaping our experiences.

One of the most significant aspects of our journey is the role of educational leadership. Educational leaders, such as principals, teachers, and policymakers, play a crucial role in shaping the policies and practices that impact our learning. Reflecting on our journey allows us to recognize the influence these leaders have had on our education, both positively and negatively. It gives us an opportunity to understand the decisions made, the strategies implemented, and the impact they had on our academic growth.

Furthermore, reflecting on our journey also enables us to recognize the broader implications of educational policy. Policies shape the educational landscape, determining everything from curriculum choices to funding allocations. Understanding these policies empowers us as students to advocate for our needs and contribute to the improvement of the education system. By reflecting on the policies we encountered throughout our journey, we can gain insights into how they impacted our experience and identify areas for improvement.

Moreover, reflecting on our journey helps us appreciate the significant milestones we have achieved. Whether it is overcoming academic challenges, embracing extracurricular activities, or developing essential life skills, acknowledging these accomplishments boosts our self-confidence and motivates us to continue striving for excellence. It reminds us that our education is not solely measured by grades and test scores, but also by the personal growth we have experienced along the way.

However, reflecting on our journey also allows us to acknowledge the struggles and setbacks we have faced. It is essential to recognize the moments when we felt overwhelmed, unsupported, or misunderstood within the education system. By acknowledging these challenges, we can gain a deeper understanding of how educational policies and leadership can play a role in addressing these issues and creating a more inclusive and supportive learning environment for all students.

In conclusion, reflecting on the journey of navigating the education system provides us with valuable insights into the role of educational leadership and policy. It allows us to recognize the influence these factors have on our education, both positive and negative, and empowers us to advocate for change. By acknowledging our achievements and challenges, we can foster personal growth and contribute to the improvement of the education system for future generations of students.

Key Takeaways and Action Steps for Students in Educational Leadership and Policy

As students interested in the field of educational leadership and policy, it is crucial to understand the key takeaways and action steps that can guide you towards success in this dynamic and important area. This subchapter aims to provide you with valuable insights and actionable advice that can help you navigate the complex world of educational leadership and policy.

1. Develop a strong foundation of knowledge: To excel in this field, it is essential to build a solid understanding of educational leadership and policy. Take advantage of the resources available to you, such as books, articles, and online courses, to deepen your knowledge. Stay updated with the latest research and trends in educational leadership and policy to ensure you are well-informed.

2. Seek mentorship and networking opportunities: Connect with professionals and experts in the field of educational leadership and policy. Seek mentorship from experienced individuals who can guide you and provide valuable insights. Attend conferences, seminars, and workshops to expand your network and gain exposure to different perspectives. Networking can open doors to internships, job opportunities, and collaborations.

3. Get involved in relevant organizations and projects: Join student organizations and clubs related to educational leadership and policy. This will give you the opportunity to collaborate with like-minded peers, engage in meaningful projects, and make a positive impact on your education community. Active involvement demonstrates your commitment and passion for the field, enhancing your credibility.

4. Gain practical experience through internships and volunteering: Look for internships or volunteer opportunities in educational institutions, government agencies, or non-profit organizations working in the field of educational leadership and policy. This hands-on experience will provide you with valuable insights into the practical aspects of implementing policies and leading educational initiatives.

5. Develop essential skills: To be effective in educational leadership and policy, you need to develop a range of skills. These include strong communication and interpersonal abilities, critical thinking and problem-solving skills, data analysis and research skills, and the ability to work collaboratively with diverse stakeholders.

6. Stay informed about policy changes and educational trends: Educational policies and trends are constantly evolving. Stay updated with the latest changes and developments in the field. Subscribe to relevant journals, newsletters, and online platforms to stay informed. Attend conferences and webinars to learn about emerging practices and innovative approaches.

7. Advocate for positive change: As a student in educational leadership and policy, you have the power to advocate for positive change in your education system. Use your voice to address issues of equity, inclusion, and quality education. Engage in discussions, write op-eds, and collaborate with others to promote policies that benefit all students.

By internalizing these key takeaways and taking action on the suggested steps, you will be well-equipped to contribute to the field of educational leadership and policy. Remember to remain curious, adaptable, and committed to lifelong learning as you navigate this exciting and impactful area.